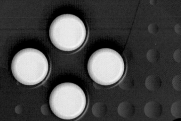

Maintaining and Upgrading a Gaming PC

21st Century Skills **INNOVATION LIBRARY**

Josh Gregory

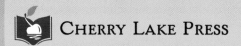
CHERRY LAKE PRESS

Published in the United States of America by Cherry Lake Publishing Group
Ann Arbor, Michigan
www.cherrylakepublishing.com

Reading Adviser: Beth Walker Gambro, MS, Ed., Reading Consultant, Yorkville, IL

Photo Credits: ©Mr.Whiskey / Shutterstock, cover, 1; ©DC Studio / Shutterstock, 5; ©Rokas Tenys, 7; ©Mny-Jhee / Shutterstock, 8; ©wavebreakmedia / Shutterstock, 9; ©Peter Gudella / Shutterstock, 11; ©KenSoftTH / Shutterstock, 12; ©stockphoto-graf / Shutterstock, 14; ©CRM / Shutterstock, 16; ©Prostock-studio / Shutterstock, 19; ©Maxx-Studio / Shutterstock, 20; ©LifeCollectionPhotography / Shutterstock, 21; ©Naumov S / Shutterstock, 23; ©P_galasso2289 / Shutterstock, 24; ©I2pTink3r / Shutterstock, 25; ©alarich / Shutterstock, 27; ©EKKAPHAN CHIMPALEE / Shutterstock, 28; ©Stanisic Vladimir / Shutterstock, 29; ©Terelyuk / Shutterstock, 31

Cherry Lake Press is an imprint of Cherry Lake Publishing Group.

Library of Congress Cataloging-in-Publication Data

Names: Gregory, Josh, author.
Title: Maintaining and upgrading a gaming PC / by Josh Gregory.
Description: Ann Arbor, Michigan : Cherry Lake Publishing, 2022. | Series:
   Unofficial guides | Series: 21st century skills innovation library |
   Includes bibliographical references and index. | Audience: Grades 4-6
   (provided by Cherry Lake Publishing)
Identifiers: LCCN 2021042779 (print) | LCCN 2021042780 (ebook) | ISBN
   9781668902240 (ebook) | ISBN 9781534199668 (library binding) | ISBN
   9781668906569 (pdf) | ISBN 9781668900802 (paperback)
Subjects: LCSH: Microcomputers—Maintenance and repair—Juvenile literature.
   | Microcomputers—Upgrading—Juvenile literature. | Computer
   games—Juvenile literature.
Classification: LCC TK7887 (ebook) | LCC TK7887 .G7347 2022 (print) | DDC
   621.39/16—dc23
LC record available at https://lccn.loc.gov/2021042779

Cherry Lake Publishing Group would like to acknowledge the work of the Partnership for 21st Century Learning, a Network of Battelle for Kids. Please visit http://www.battelleforkids.org/networks/p21 for more information.

Printed in the United States of America
Corporate Graphics

Josh Gregory is the author of more than 125 books for kids. He has written about everything from animals to technology to history. A graduate of the University of Missouri–Columbia, he currently lives in Chicago, Illinois.

Contents

CHAPTER 1

However You Want to Play

How do you like to play video games? Do you like to tap on a phone or a tablet? Or do you prefer to sit on a couch with a controller in your hand? Maybe you like games to push the limits of graphics technology. Or perhaps you prefer the old-school charms of retro games. There are all kinds of different games available, and all kinds of ways to enjoy them.

If you're really serious about gaming, you might even want to play in a really specific way. Maybe you want a machine more powerful than even the latest PlayStation or Xbox video game consoles. Or maybe you want a gaming setup made specially for driving games, complete with a steering wheel, pedals, and racing seat. Or a high-end virtual reality (VR) system. Or a device that looks like an old arcade machine but is packed with hundreds of classic games. If any of these things sounds interesting, you might want to become a PC gamer.

PC gaming is all about choice and customization. You can put together any kind of gaming system, use any kinds of controllers, and play on any kind of screen. You can design a custom system that matches the rest of your room or pack the parts into a tiny box that easily hides out of sight. And when it's time to actually play games, you can choose exactly how they will run. Do

If you want the most advanced graphics, the latest VR tech, or other high-end features, PC gaming is the only way to go.

Build or Buy?

One of the biggest questions most people face when they decide to get into PC gaming is whether to buy a pre-built computer or build one from scratch. There are advantages and disadvantages to each. If you buy a PC, you don't have to worry about making mistakes or ending up with parts that don't work correctly. You might also get a warranty from the company that built it. However, you won't get to customize as many details of your new machine.

Building your own PC is not as hard as it sounds. Modern PC parts are often color coded, and many of them can snap together without using any tools. Many PC builders compare it to putting a LEGO set together. Building your own PC gives you the chance to tweak every tiny detail. It can also teach you a lot about how PCs work and what different parts do. The biggest downside is that you might end up needing to solve problems on your own. However, even this can be an important learning experience. The more time you spend working with PC hardware, the better you will understand it.

you want the fastest possible **frame rate**? Or would you rather see the most detailed, high-**resolution** graphics? Every detail is up to you.

Most game systems make most of these background decisions for you. For example, if you are on a

Newer consoles such as the PlayStation 5 offer more graphical settings than older systems did, but they are still not nearly as flexible as a PC.

PlayStation or an Xbox, you might get to choose between two or three graphical settings. On a PC, the same game might let you tweak dozens of different options. There is a downside to all of this freedom, though. With more options, there are more possibilities for problems. And in many cases, you'll need to fix those problems yourself.

For most PC gamers, fixing computer problems and getting things to run just the right way are part of the fun. PC gaming is a hobby that attracts people who love to tinker, try new things, and keep up to date with the latest technology. Even when they aren't playing games, they are updating their machines and planning their next **upgrade**.

One great thing about a gaming PC is that it can last for years and years if you take care of it. Just like a classic car, it takes a little maintenance to keep things

Learning how the different parts of a PC fit together is easier than you might think.

Basic tools like screwdrivers and pliers are all you will need to work on a modern PC.

running smoothly. And unlike many modern devices, you don't need to replace it if it breaks down. With the right knowledge and some simple tools, you can fix it up and get right back in the game!

CHAPTER 2

Taking Care of Your PC

Every day, there are things you do to keep yourself healthy, clean, and feeling good. You sleep at night. You wash yourself and brush your teeth. You eat when you're hungry and get your hair cut when it grows too long. If you don't do these things, it can have a negative impact on your life. Similarly, a PC that gets regular care and maintenance will last longer and run more smoothly than a neglected PC.

If you set things up the right way, a lot of basic PC maintenance will happen automatically. Digital game stores like Steam and the Epic Games store will automatically download **patches** and other updates for your games. Your **operating system** will download major updates for the **software** that makes your computer run. Often, you can even choose to install programs that will keep each individual part of your computer up to date. For example, most video cards allow you to install an app that will automatically update **drivers** when needed. This is especially helpful when you are playing brand-new, recently released games. Often, video card manufacturers create new drivers when a highly anticipated new game is released. These drivers ensure that your video card will be ready for the new game.

Sometimes you might need to download and install an update manually. This usually means going to a

The latest video card drivers usually feature special fixes to make newly released games run better.

website, finding the file you need, downloading it, and then going through the installation process. It is usually pretty simple. But anytime you update or change any software on your computer, there is a chance that it will cause a problem. This is just a fact of life when it comes to PCs. Sometimes you might be able to fix these kinds of problems by changing some settings in one of your programs. Other times, you might need to

Make sure you unplug your PC from the power supply on the back of the machine before you start working.

wait for another update to be released and fix the problems caused by the previous one.

Are you curious to see exactly how well your PC is performing? There are all kinds of programs that can show you how hard the different parts of your computer are working at different times. For example, does your CPU have to run at top speed all the time

Safety First

Be careful anytime you open up your PC to clean it or work inside. Before you do anything, make sure the PC is shut down and the switch on the power supply is turned off. You should also unplug the power cable from the back of the machine. Doing these things will prevent you from getting shocked. You should also keep an eye out for sharp edges or pointy bits of metal inside your PC case. These can easily scratch or poke you. Try to avoid pinching your fingers when you are snapping pieces into place or opening and closing latches. None of these things are likely to give you a serious injury, but they can definitely hurt!

when you play games? Or can it handle things comfortably? More importantly, are you getting the results you want from your games? One way to judge this is simply to play games and determine for yourself if they feel smooth and look good. But if you want to measure more accurately, keep an eye on the frame rate. Steam and similar programs can display a game's frame rate in the corner of the screen as you play. Many PC gamers aim for a frame rate of at least 60. This means the computer is changing the image on

Some PC players put a lot of work into making their fan setups look nice while functioning correctly.

your screen 60 times per second. The higher the number, the smoother the movement on screen will be. In generally, most people agree that anything below 30 frames per second can start to make it difficult to enjoy a game. However, different people have different tastes and opinions. Some PC gamers insist on very high frame rates, while others are happy to play at lower ones if it means they can crank up the graphics settings.

You can get programs that help you keep an eye on the temperatures inside your PC. The harder your PC has to run, the more heat it will create. This means you have to have a good cooling system in place. Most of the time, this will be a set of fans inside your PC case arranged to suck in cool air from outside and push out hot air from inside. Fans can be plugged into your PC's motherboard and then set up to spin at different speeds depending on how hard the computer is working. Fans can make a lot of noise, though. Some PC builders prefer to set up liquid cooling systems. These systems run tubes of liquid through the computer. The liquid absorbs heat as it moved through a loop. It then passes through a device that cools it down. The cooled liquid passes back through the loop and absorbs more heat, and this cycle is repeated

If you see something like this when you open your PC, take the time to clean up, then consider if there's something you can do to improve the airflow in your machine.

over and over. This type of system can be pricey and difficult to set up. However, it is much quieter than a normal fan-based cooling system.

One important and often overlooked form of PC maintenance is cleaning. Every once in a while, open up your PC case to see if it is dusty. Remember that fans will pull air in from the room outside the case. If the room is dusty or full of pet hair, these things can make your PC dirty. A dirty, dusty PC is more likely to get hot inside. Use a cloth to wipe the outside of the case. Pay careful attention to any vents or other openings. Inside the case, use canned compressed air to blow away any dust that has settled.

One way to make it easier to clean the inside of your PC is to make sure you don't have any loose wires or other parts dangling all over. Try to organize all the wires and cables in your case to be as neat and organized as possible. Many modern PC cases have all kinds of built-in features to help you keep wires organized. You can also use wire ties to group wires together and keep them held out of the way. The fewer places there are for dust to gather, the cleaner your PC will be.

CHAPTER 3

Making Changes

No matter how well you take of it, your PC will eventually start to fall behind the times. This is OK if you only want to play older games or use the same old programs. But if you want to stay up to date, you'll eventually need to upgrade your hardware.

You don't need to have built your PC from scratch to upgrade its hardware. In fact, you can swap out parts on just about any Windows-based desktop PC. If you play games on a laptop or a Mac, you'll have far fewer upgrade options. However, depending on the exact computer you have, you might be able to do basic things like adding more **memory** or increasing the size of your hard drive.

If you are like most PC gamers and are using a Windows desktop machine, then the sky is the limit when it comes to upgrades. You will be able to change just about any detail of your PC that you want. As a result, the first step of any upgrading project is simply to decide what you want to do. Do you want to make minor changes to give your current setup a little boost? Or do you want to gut your machine and start mostly from scratch? The answer will depend on what you are hoping to achieve by upgrading.

A laptop can be a great way to play PC games, but you will have far fewer options for upgrading.

Some upgrades are very simple. For example, maybe you're noticing that your hard drive is close to filling up. If you don't want to start uninstalling games or deleting files, you'll need to add more hard drive space. You don't need to replace anything to do this. All you need to do is open up your PC, install another hard drive, and make sure it is correctly attached to your motherboard. Most cases have room for several hard drives, so you are unlikely to run out of space for new ones.

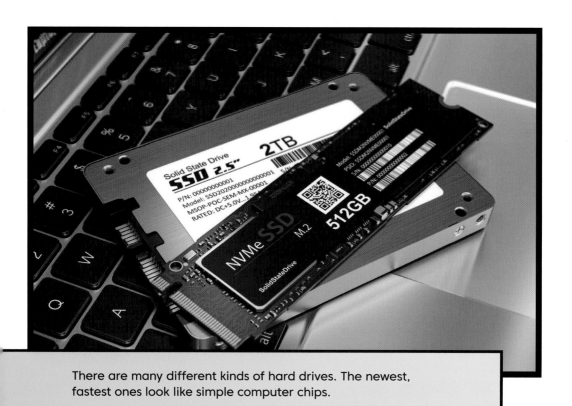

There are many different kinds of hard drives. The newest, fastest ones look like simple computer chips.

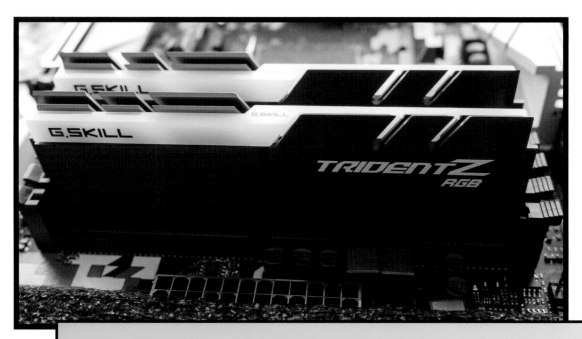

Even if you don't have any experience working on PCs, it is very easy to install memory.

Similarly, if there are open slots on your motherboard, you can add more memory. This can make it easier for your PC to run certain games, or to keep multiple programs running at the same time.

Maybe you are noticing that your PC is struggling to reach high frame rates without turning down the graphical settings on new games. Or, even worse, maybe your machine isn't even meeting the minimum system requirements for the games you want to play. In these cases, you might need to swap out some of the main parts of your PC, such as your **processor** or video card. Video card upgrades are usually fairly easy. All you need to do is remove the old card and plug in the new one. Then you need to make sure your PC has the right driver for the new card. A new video card is often the most powerful upgrade you can make when it comes to gaming.

Building on a Budget

PC hardware can be very expensive, especially if you want the latest and greatest technology. Unless you have a lot of money to spare, it doesn't make much sense to upgrade every time a shiny new PC part is released. But even if you are only upgrading once in a while, it is easy to spend a lot of money on new parts.

It's a good idea to set a strict budget for yourself when it comes to PC upgrades. For example, try deciding on a maximum amount you can spend on PC parts each year. Then stay below that number! Remember to leave yourself some room in your budget for emergencies. You don't want to blow all of your funds on a new video card, only to have your power supply break down a week later. Also, try to only make upgrades you really need. The newest hardware can be tempting, but it might not always offer a huge advantage over your current setup.

Upgrading your processor can be a little more complex than other changes. A new processor will often require a new motherboard. This means you will have to take most of the computer apart to make the upgrade. And speaking of motherboards, you'll almost never want to replace yours unless you really have to. Changing to a new motherboard while keeping all your other parts is

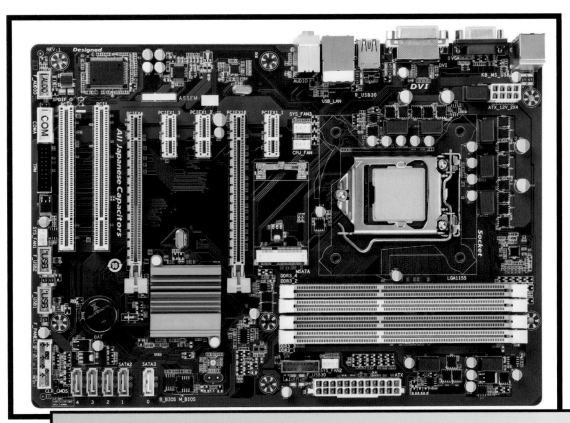

A motherboard acts as a central location for all of your other parts to connect, but it does not do much of the heavy lifting when it comes to running a game.

A fast processor is very important for running the latest games.

generally not going to make your games run any better.

Sometimes, swapping out a part or two just isn't enough. Maybe your computer has gotten seriously out of date. Or maybe you are having a hard time finding new parts that are **compatible** with what you already have. In these cases, you might need to start almost from scratch. However, you probably don't need to start *all* the way from nothing. Things like your case, power supply, cooling system, and maybe even your hard drives could all be used in the new build. This will save you a lot of money compared to building an entirely new PC. Always check to see what you can keep as you move forward with new hardware.

Even if you have to replace all the main components of your PC, you will rarely have to rebuild every single part of the machine from scratch.

CHAPTER 4

Thinking Ahead

One of the main things you'll need to consider before making an upgrade is compatibility. Not every new PC part will work with the ones you already have. Be careful to check carefully before purchasing a new piece of hardware. If you built your own PC, one great resource is the instruction manual that came with your motherboard. It will tell you exactly which kinds of parts will connect to it. Another thing to watch out for is your power supply. If you try adding a bunch of powerful new parts, you need to make sure you can supply them with the amount of electricity they need to run. Many PC builders get a stronger power supply than they need when putting a new machine together. This makes it easier to upgrade in the future.

The other big thing to think about is avoiding bottlenecks. A bottleneck is when a piece of hardware can't reach its full potential because of the other parts in the system. For example, imagine you have a computer that is a few years old, and you want to replace the video card. The latest, fastest video card might technically be compatible with your computer. But the actual results it gives you might not be any better than you could get from a slightly less powerful card. In other words, try to avoid a situation where any of the main parts in your PC are much more powerful

The more powerful your PC is, the more likely it is to need more electricity.

or much weaker than the others. It won't stop your PC from working correctly, but it is a big waste of money.

If you really get into building and upgrading PCs, it can be very helpful to set up a permanent workspace where you can tinker with hardware and store your supplies. Ideally, you will have a big, flat surface like a desk, table, or countertop where you can lay your PC as you work. If your PC is already on a desk, you can work in

A good, clean workspace can make tinkering with your machine and playing games even more enjoyable.

If you think you might sell a part later on, consider keeping its original box.

the same space you play games. This is good because you don't need to move your PC around much when you need to work on it.

Never throw old PC parts away after upgrading. It can be useful to hang on to them in case you need spare parts in the future. Many PC gamers also like to sell or trade their old parts when upgrading. This gives them more room in their budget for better upgrades. If you do end up with old parts that truly have no use anymore, you still shouldn't throw them out. Like all electronic devices, they should be donated to an electronics recycling center. Throwing PC parts in the trash is not just wasteful, but also bad for the environment.

Pushed Past the Limit

If you really like to tinker, there is another way to get more power out of your PC. Through a process called overclocking, you can increase the speed of your processor or video card beyond their normal settings. Overclocking is not very complicated once you know what you are doing. However, it is not for beginners. You'll need to do some reading and possibly watch some tutorial videos online to get a handle on the process before you start.

One thing to keep in mind: overclocking can cause PC parts to malfunction if you don't do it right. Overclocked parts will get hotter than they normally would. This can cause them to shut down and stop working. Usually they will not be permanently damaged. However, overclocked parts have a higher chance of failing in the long run, since they are running harder. A good cooling system can really help if you decide to try it for yourself.

Don't forget to enjoy all your hard work once you get your PC set up just right.

Are you ready to start tinkering with your own PC? Soon, you might be having so much fun upgrading and tweaking your machine that you forget to play any games!

GLOSSARY

compatible (kuhm-PAT-i-buhl) able to work together

drivers (DRY-vurz) computer programs that control a specific piece of hardware, such as a video card or a mouse

frame rate (FRAYM RAYT) a measurement of how many times per second the image on screen changes when playing a game

hardware (HARD-wair) the physical parts that make up a computer

memory (MEM-uh-ree) a device that is able to hold information for later use

operating system (AH-pur-ay-ting SIS-tuhm) a program, such as Microsoft Windows or macOS, that controls the functions of a computer

patches (PATCH-es) updates to a game or other computer program that are created after the program is released

processor (PRAH-sess-ur) the central "brain" of a computer that processes information

resolution (rez-uh-LOO-shuhn) a measurement of how detailed an image is

software (SAWFT-wair) computer programs

upgrade (UP-grayd) to replace something with a better version

warranty (WOR-uhn-tee) an agreement from a company or store to repair or replace defective products within a certain period of time

FIND OUT MORE

Books

Cunningham, Kevin. *Video Game Designer*. Ann Arbor, MI: Cherry Lake Publishing, 2016.

Loh-Hagan, Virginia. *Video Games*. Ann Arbor, MI: Cherry Lake Publishing, 2021.

Powell, Marie. *Asking Questions About Video Games*. Ann Arbor, MI: Cherry Lake Publishing, 2016.

Websites

Logical Increments

www.logicalincrements.com/

This incredibly useful website will help you find parts that work well together and see how much they cost.

INDEX